WAITING FOR BLUEBEARD

Helen Ivory was born in Luton in 1969 and began to write poems at Norwich School of Art in 1997, under the tuition of George Szirtes. She won an Eric Gregory Award in 1999 and then disappeared into a field in the Norfolk countryside to look after two thousand free-range hens. When she emerged ten or so years later, she had two collections with Bloodaxe Books and had helped, with her own bare hands, to build several houses.

She is a poet and artist, a freelance creative writing tutor and course director for creative writing for continuing education at the University of East Anglia, an editor for The Poetry Archive, editor of the webzine *Ink Sweat and Tears*, and co-organiser with Martin Figura of Café Writers in Norwich.

She has published four collections with Bloodaxe Books, *The Double Life of Clocks* (2002), *The Dog in the Sky* (2006), *The Breakfast Machine* (2010) and *Waiting for Bluebeard* (2013). She was awarded an Arts Council writer's bursary in 2005 and an Author's Foundation Grant in 2008.

Her website is www.helenivory.co.uk

HELEN IVORY

WAITING FOR BLUEBEARD

for Philip

*thank you
for buying this
book!*

*warmest wishes
Helen*

BLOODAXE BOOKS

ISBN: 978 1 85224 975 5

First published 2013 by
Bloodaxe Books Ltd,
Highgreen,
Tarset,
Northumberland NE48 1RP.

www.bloodaxebooks.com
For further information about Bloodaxe titles
please visit our website or write to
the above address for a catalogue.

Supported by
**ARTS COUNCIL
ENGLAND**

Cover art: Helen Ivory (photograph: Martin Figura)

Cover design: Neil Astley & Pamela Robertson-Pearce.

Printed in Great Britain by
Bell & Bain Limited, Glasgow, Scotland.

*In memory of grandmothers Annie Florence and Nora Daisy,
my cousin Emma Jane, my aunties Winnie and Joyce.*

*This book is dedicated to all of the women who have
spent time inside Bluebeard's house.*

*The house was a snow globe,
and each time we landed
we found ourselves altered.*

CONTENTS

PART TWO

PART ONE

Moon Landing

Somewhere beyond weather
men are reckoning the acreage of space
and playing tricks on gravity.

My pregnant mother watches with the millions
in their front rooms as she waits
but I will not budge.

Meanwhile the men, wrapped inside their skins,
trust their lives to science
and whatever wonder brought them there.

The suitcase has been packed for days.
All the clothes are white or lemon.
A man plays hopscotch on the moon.

My mother's wedding dress

was a spun-sugar confection
and her bouquet made of helicopters,
plastic zoo animals,
little dogs that ran on batteries,
and every sort of household thing
you could think of.

Behind the bouquet,
a baby moved in a bell jar
like a cosmonaut testing space.

What the Moon Said

If you send me your jumping cows,
your space rockets
peopled by monkeys and dogs,
I will flatter you with my light.

And if you compose tunes,
I will choreograph
the bodies of the sky
for your delectation.

Cut open your church roof
let me drink milk
from a bowl on your floor.

First Born

After a picnic in the park
my mother gave birth to an egg.
At the hospital they placed it in an incubator
and the midwives held vigil.

Her mother said
it was the tuna paste being 'off'
and didn't believe the fanciful story
involving the swan and the roundabout.

On the day of the hatching
the sun rose as usual and my grandmother
took her customary bus to the hospital
with grapes and Lucozade.

The next day my mother took her bundle home,
oblivious of the entourage of swans
massing in the sky above the bus.
The baby looked like any other newborn.

A Beginning

While my mother was washing up
I formed in a bubble
that rose to the top of the bowl.

I had many sisters,
but none of them made it whole
to the surface world.

I drifted to the middle of the room
and settled on the light bulb
which was mercifully off.

My mother didn't notice me
till I was covered in cobwebs
and had begun to form words in my throat.

The Stolen Babies

My mother's babies
were undoable knots
stolen from her womb
by the fairies, she said.

She pitied the fairies,
being from the otherworld
they couldn't breed young
of their own.

When my sister was born
the cat had kittens too;
blind, shaky, seeming
not quite set on this world.

We never left her alone
with these creatures
lest they sneaked her away
all parcelled in fur.

Nights

Those sleepless nights of my childhood
where cats and phantom cats
hiss from opposing corners of the room,
where the moon somehow rests
on the top of the wardrobe.

And voices haul themselves
up the stairwell
to stand awkward in the doorway,
or else chase each other
down the street with knives.

What the Dark Said

The dark prefers to listen,
has much buried away
in its drawers and under its tongue:

the rusted knife; the christening gown,
the apple seeds sewn in its hem;
a chronicle of undelivered letters.

The dark likes not to get involved,
holds stars and planets
loosely in its arms as they dance.

But when the dark clears its throat
dogs and wolves look down from the sky
and the four winds race from their caves.

Playing House

I am constructing a house
from cardboard and fabric
and bits of flowery wallpaper

while my mother sings
the song of a girl
as she skips with a rope.

There is a black and white cat
skit-skattering round the hall
with a cotton reel.

The walls are held together
with sellotape and the roof
is an upside-down box.

And the bed that I've made
from a matchbox is big enough
for only my smallest doll

who is hairless now, and almost
eyeless; who has the head
of a child, the body of a woman.

My Mother's Room

She is uncertain if the room
is the hidden architecture of sleep
or if its walls are made of real plaster and straw.

So she walks the house every night,
along corridors that vanish like thieves
soon after the sun appears.

There is a singing that shines from a closed door
but with hands turned to fishes
she can't move the handle.

There is a kind of singing that turns winter on its hinge,
that wakes animals from their long sleep
and places birds on the highest shelf of the sky.

My mother listens intently,
but with her ears turned to caves,
it's all echoes.

What the Stars Said

Following a long afternoon of reflection
the stars no longer believed
they were sheep, waiting for a midnight field.

They grew fearful of heights,
enquired of the little girl as she prayed:
May we hide in your room?

So they flocked to her tiny house,
heaved themselves under her bed
and began to burn holes in the rug.

Drive

It is true that people stopped
wearing hats
soon after the car was invented
and that my hatless mother
failed her test the year her father died.

It was something to do with gears
something that later
my father tried to fix
till she was too pregnant
to fit behind the wheel.

On family holidays
we would have to stop often
for her to breathe,
my father pulling into lay-bys,
she clutching tissues to her mouth.

I can see her outline now
moving away from the car,
headscarf drawn against a sky
that could easily have fallen in,
according to chicken in the tale.

Paper

It is easier to make her daughters matching clothes, thinks my mother as she cuts out patterns from a pattern book. She has made some triangles for skirts which when pieced together will be upside down flowerpots. Very soon her girls will stand hand in hand cut from the same piece of paper stretched out to the horizon with the trees.

Crafts

*

I don't remember when my mother used to make rugs,
but I recall them smothering the lino.
I do remember the candles settling into their moulds
and their wicks sticking up like drowning hands.

And the images made from nails and silk
describing boats and flowers
in spirograph curves
tensed over black hessian.

*

For my first-year needlework class
I failed to make the shape of a frog from a pattern,
so I lay awake through the chunter of her sewing-machine
as she joined the two halves.

In the morning
I filled it with dried pulses
and tried to suture
the gap she'd left at its crown.

Things My Mother Never Told Me

The earth is flat and can be divided
into slices like a pie.
Days are like toy theatres
and anything could happen in them.

And if a snake curls itself on the floor,
that no amount of coaxing will cast it back
into the space and no manner of paint
will cover these uneven surfaces.

And sometimes, even a simple cotton reel
can hold every thread of your being
wound up so neat,
you might never see you again.

Take. From. Away.
A lesson in mathematics
(after Louise Richardson)

If a person is the sum of her parts
then let there be no more of me.
Unhinge my ribs, unbutton my vertebrae,
pull each slow thread
till I am spider-writing on a gridded page.

And whatever wretched work
is made of these subtractions,
mark it with your reddest pen, teacher.
Here, I will draw my own stars;
clothe myself in the ripped-out pages of this book.

Bird Fish

The goldfish in the garden are buried in matchbox coffins; tiny bones finer than cat whiskers. When it rains hard, the girl imagines them all born to a new life underground, doing a kind of half-swim in the mud. The buried birds will also be reborn wide-eyed and featherless, to a time before breathing. Then the girl wonders what became of the kittens – bones too fragile to hold their pelts; hearts too anxious to escape their cages.

The Family at Night

We were rag-dolls after school
and passed long winter evenings like this:
father in his armchair with an unlit pipe,
mother in the kitchen pretending to eat,
my sister and I with our small occupations.

We saw little with our button eyes
and spoke even less with our stitched-up mouths.
We played at playing till it was time for bed
when mother sewed our eyelids down
so we could get a good night's rest.

We always woke as our human selves
to find the downstairs rooms had altered too.
A chair unstuffed, a table's legs all wrong,
and, that one time, kittens gone from their basket;
the mother's bone-hollow meow.

Sunday Morning

It all comes back to the breakfast table
still set in the middle of a room
which has become so vast and arid
you would need a camel train to cross it.

Her father has turned himself
into wallpaper, and is rolling further
and further up the wall,
away from the sidewinders in the carpet.

There is the Sunday smell of washing powder
and the glimpse of her mother's back
as she pegs out uniforms
in the oasis of grass in a far corner.

She is doing her best to spoon marmalade
onto her toast, but it is molten in the desert sun.
A solitary crumb falls from the table
and a snake sidles over, all eyes.

What the Cat Said

Empty your past lives
onto the table,
let me chase them away like mice.

I will catch one,
turn it neat inside out –
see, the mouse has no heart.

And when we've finished
tidying up,
each skull licked perfectly clean,

we can set about building
a nest fit for catlings
from the fur drifts under your bed.

Jonah the Giant Whale

When the tour came to Luton
it was thirty years dead
and had forgotten
about blood and the sea.

Its mouth was wedged open
but there were no fish to be had,
only school children
with heads full of stories.

The drone of its heart
charged the tent
with a chemical winter,
made us hunch into our cardigans.

For a while I kept the ticket;
a picture of a whale
which a man ripped the tail from
as I passed through the turnstile.

Trampoline

My sister and I are on trampolines
and have been warned
to keep to the X.

If we jump high enough
we can see the sea which for its part,
seems to be going the wrong way.

A bucket of windmills
blurs against
the steady breeze

and I catch the eye of a gull
who seems also to have noticed
the strange behaviour of the sea.

It begins to laugh
as I try to steady myself
on the X.

What the Sea Said

I am the eyes and tongues of the hundred-year dead
I am the weight of the sky
I am spilling from your picture book.

You are a child in the belly of a stone
a small boat emptied of its fish
a story picked clean to its bones.

And when the sea sat down to listen
the morning was as night
and gulls hurried to the roosting cliffs.

My Father and the Sand Boat

There are two seats
and when the tide comes in
we will make our journey
with the plastic oars
we found in the sand.

Almost out of earshot
a tinny sound system
is wasting its breath
while here, an inflated chicken
looms over the dunes.

The oars are kind of runcible
and it's tricky to tell
what use they'll be
if the sea takes us away,
though it's showing no signs.

Late

The dark street
with half-hearted
lamps hovering,
just overhead.

My mother
has topped up the water
in the steamer
three times.

She looks out
of the window,
at the snow
that's encroaching.

What the Snow Said

Saints watch open-eyed
as I plenty the air
with intolerable light.

*

You scoop handfuls
of flesh,
moulding me in your image.

*

You wished for me,
guided me here
with prayer and with song.

*

Gravestones peer
from my hands
like rotten teeth.

*

Go to sleep child,
I will free the world
of its clanking.

Chameleon

My mother kept a chameleon instead of a dog and when I was at school it did the job of passing notes to my father. It was very clever at appearing anywhere around the house – hanging by its tail from the curtain pole, materialising suddenly from the pattern of the armchair. The quickness of its eyes meant he never got away, and when its elastic tongue delivered the message somewhere between temple and cheek, it would always come with the clatter of pans from down the hall, or the angry whiz of a blender.

Creature

Because I wanted to be a horse when I grew up
my mother let me roam the streets at night.

I wore slippers on my hooves
to stop their clitter-clat waking the neighbours.

Once a school friend, a fanciful girl,
said she saw a deer in wasteland outside school

and kept everyone back at hometime
looking into every corner of dark.

Bird

When the cat came home
with a mouthful of feathers
and *that* look in his eye,
for once, the bird was still alive.

We nursed it best we could, mashed bread,
prayed solemnly to the God of Broken Things,
but its frightened heart
was too swift, too fleet for this world.

We cleared a patch of snow for the funeral,
dug a spade-deep hole for the matchbox coffin
and sang *All Things Bright and Beautiful*
in high, warbling church-like voices.

Trinity

My coterie still follows me;
the emu, the bear, the hedgehog,
now nesting mice in their bellies.

They stand directly behind me in mirrors;
shadow me though parks,
pretending to be leaves and songbirds.

On cold days they unzip their skins;
dress me up in fur, to protect me
from the apple-head doll's shrivelled smirk.

And as I climb back into the wardrobe
they stand brave in their nakedness,
armed with paring knives, dessert spoons.

Mrs Day

She'd left parts of herself everywhere
and when she was very old,
tended the small carnivorous garden
on her windowsill.

You could see her deft hands
removing the undigested skeletons
of flies from green throats
with a pair of tweezers.

All the mean stray dogs
in the street were her children
and at night she would call them
like a moon coaxing the sea.

Only one person, a girl from the agency,
ever went in to her flat
with baskets of food, snags of lace, bone and fur,
collected from all over town.

Red Coat

Autumn, feeling more like winter,
the sky impeccably dark,
save the artillery of fireworks
from a neighbour's garden,

and here I am, trapped on the roof
of my grandmother's coal-bunker
by a nasty little puppy
with pin-tacks for teeth.

And as the story goes,
I am wearing a bright red coat,
but I have already given him
all the treats from my basket.

When the fireworks stop
I hear the late night chime
of the town hall clock
and the puppy, gruffling the dark.

Quarantine

I am shut in my bedroom
in a pale lemon bridesmaid dress
on the afternoon of the royal wedding.

Skin blotched with calamine,
I am an invisible listener
as the world makes trifle.

Since the start of my quarantine,
I have been training magpies
to do my bidding

but they all flew away
when they heard the silver band
tuning up at the end of the road.

So I have gathered my coterie
round an upturned milk-crate
for a celebration tea of plasticine cakes.

It is a while since we dined together
and strictly *entre nous*,
their table manners aren't as they were.

But outside now, my magpies have come
to their senses, and gather over the heads
of the street party.

One for sorrow, two for mirth,
Three for a wedding, four for a birth,
Five for silver, six for gold,
Seven for a secret not to be told.

The Paper Bag Man

In that nightmare
where a man made of paper
stands at the bottom of the stairs
with pages for arms
and paper bags for hands

he is unpeeling the woodchip
my parents pasted up
one summer holiday;
winding it around himself
masquerading as a corpse.

Of course there is nothing
to be afraid of,
nothing in his head
but empty breezes
the paperboy lets in when he calls.

Sick Bed

Creature
swaddled in eider;
cocooned,
waiting for my wings.

Burning up,
I am wood turned charcoal,
I am drawing
all over the walls.

Graffiti child,
I have made a map of me
but I am out
of land.

I kick at the uncharted walls,
to test
if they are sea
or starry air.

What the Bed Said

White quilt, smotherer
dream-murderer
blindfolder of my days.

I have carried fish-babies
right here in my belly,
born them far into the earth-wide sky.

I have held a woman
in my breath
till only an ounce of her was left.

Yet how can I speak
when my tongue is cushioned
by your mother-love?

The Story of the Shed

When his daughters were very small, my father built them a shed right at the bottom of the garden. The shed was no ordinary shed, it was made from wooden pallets and four inch nails. It was doorless. The wood was green and still bled in places, in others skin and teeth were flaking away, ripe for splinters and snags. One day the shed bit his eldest on the heel of her hand so fierce, a splinter lodged deep in her flesh. Try as she might, no needle would free it, not even a pin from her grandmother's toolbox. She is sleeping still. When she wakes, she will be a harbour for all the lost birds. She will be a living tree.

My Two Fathers

When my father removes his skin
he steps to one side and tidies
the old skin away with a dustpan and brush.

He wants nothing more
than not to make a spectacle,
but my mother insists he fill it with stones.

The stone father is anchored
to the armchair, while the other
goes upstairs to his room in a sulk.

The stone father holds the television control,
orchestrates the night's entertainment.
The other stays asleep like a bear.

Oil

My father lived beneath cars
and his blood was the measure of oil.
His meals were passed under
and cups were returned with prints,
good enough to catch any thief.

A hundred years later
my mother left with the carthorse,
the glass clowns, a suitcase
full of babies' teeth
and all the records in the house.

My father's cars were skeletons;
emptied of their hearts
hollowed of their eyes and tongues.
He cried oil, bled oil, drowned in oil,
or so the legend goes.

Her Father's Sketchbooks

were filled with galleons
and scalding sunsets,
with careful studies
of his family.

His silences flooded
the house with ink;
his voice was the grazing
of graphite on paper.

Night Shift

My father was a shadow
who stood at the school gates
fresh from the factory
where he'd pieced cars together all night.

His old-fashioned clothes
were oil-stained and solder-burnt,
and his face wore the aspect
of moonless dark.

One winter, the north wind
pushed me right through him.
It was like losing your way
in the hills, in the rain.

My Father's Accident

By then he had stopped painting us
so I picked up his book,
turned it upside-down
and filled up the last pages.

I couldn't see the absence of floor,
the way the furniture floated on rafts
in a sea of lava,
so I painted in carpet round his chair.

Nor could I see his dead father
beating his stick like a metronome
against the ceiling,
nor the broken bones of his dog.

What I did see was the sketch of a man,
head held together with spiders' legs
and the smell of the hospital
still trapped in his clothes.

Her Uncle's New House

Her parents had gone there for serious talks
but the dumb waiter spent all night
conveying food though the storeys.

The head of a pig, cooked till its eyes
were cataract milky, jaw fallen open
to a wise-cracking grin.

A rabbit blancmange wobbling
through each jolt of the hoist,
fiercely trying to keep a straight face.

The Butchery

By the time I was ten
I went to the Butchery alone
with a five pound note wrapped up
in a shopping list
inside my mother's basket.

I always saw the pheasants first,
tied up at the ankle,
the empty screens of their eyes
clocking me as I dragged myself past,
my shoes turned to glue.

When I passed my list to Mr Lingly,
he would move his hands over
the inside-out animals on the counter
picking out eviscerated bits
to match my mothers' writing.

On the walk home
I thought of the thinly sliced tongue
sealed up in wax paper,
of the empty pelt I glimpsed
through a door at the back of the shop.

I still had the list in my hand,
with his blood fingerprints all over it.
The one thing not crossed off:
a line of illegible whorls
with an ink question mark at the end.

Séance Night

Monday night was séance night
in our tiny council house
when great uncles and aunts rode by
on the carousel of voices
that passed my mother's lips.

Once a stranger claimed he was
the spirit of my father's father
and took the voice of my mother
for the whole sitting,
bragging he was a hangman
in the country's last gallows.

The lampshade in my bedroom
wore a fringe fashioned into tiny nooses
that spilled shadows on the woodchip.
I said the Lord's Prayer
as I lay down to sleep
and night muscled up to the window.

Her Wedding Ring

When she washed up
she placed it on the window sill
where it lay – ghost of the moon
among the soap suds.

It had grown so thin
that one night wolves and dogs
began their song to darkness
in the soapy cosmos.

The Story of Fire

After fire had ripped though the trees and towns and had left skeletons of houses and furniture, it turned its attentions on the graveyard. All my dead are there, neat in boxes, and fire skipped over their graves singing. When the song could not wake them, it pushed and shoved at the stones, but they would not budge. Once fire had squandered its strength on the stones, it shrank to the size of a single flame, which my mother blew out with a goodnight kiss.

My Grandmother's Lodger

She used her hand-cranked machine,
while Death whizzed ahead with electricity.
They sat at the same table, and when she made tea
he took it stewed with three sugars.

He was quicker on straight runs,
was a genius at pillowcases and curtains
while she sewed the eyes onto dolls
and lace onto petticoats with a dexterity he envied.

Since he'd taken her husband
Death had acquired the cold side of the bed,
liked nothing more than watching her sleep;
coveted her breathing, even her dreams.

His insomnia always drove him downstairs
where he would sew too many sheets
for the sleeping, the rest he would sell
at the church jumble sale.

The Hypnotist

My uncle was a hypnotist
in a rundown part of town.
His hands were birds,
passing over clients heads,
and moving in the swim of air
around them.

One time, he sat for hours,
the warmth of his palms
resting on the closed eyes of a blind girl,
while a projectionist inside her head
fired up movies of the apocalypse,
and the horsemen's winning smiles.

Another 3 a.m. Call

Every night, my grandmother
rehearses her journey
into the otherworld
as her womenfolk stand by,
rooted to this world by strong cups of tea.

The air is electricity
and it's easy to imagine
my grandmother's travels
and how superfluous
slippers might be.

We dress her in her wedding gown,
her auburn hair with violets.
On the walk home
night fits around us
like a freshly torn coat.

Yellow Fields

The young man cried for his mother
all his last night,
my grandmother says.

She is sewing rag dolls
in bloomers for the raffle,
listening to the records
an Irish man left her;
all the friends that she makes
keep dying.

On the day of the fête, it's raining
and fairy cakes are covered by clingfilm,
their hundreds and thousands bleed
into the white icing.

This metaphor is too gloomy.
Instead, let's see an August day,
a drive back from a visit
to her new country house,
fields of rapeseed, brighter than anything.

Bride

My mother's mother
was the thirteenth child
of a thirteenth child.

Her bones were made
of blown glass
and her wedding day flowers
borrowed from a grave.

The night her husband died
she saw his soul
leave his body and fade
like an unfixed daguerreotype.

Hospital Visit

The waiting room is full
of all sorts, pretending
to be awake.

The bad mother,
deaf ear cocked
to the incubator;

the bogey man,
painted eyeballs on his hands,
wedged upright in the corner.

Even the alchemist
has discovered a way
to shoe horses in his sleep.

Ward

The first visit you were seen through,
examined on slides,
your soft tissues photographed
and hung up to dry like washing.

By the second they had found
what they were looking for.
There was a cupboard for your clothes
and a bowl for apples.

After the third, you didn't wish for a fourth,
so were sent home with notes.
We bought you pretty pyjamas
and an old-fashioned pillbox.

I can still see the sun
crammed into your room every morning,
leaching lemon paint
from your bedside table.

My Grandmother and Mrs Crow

While she was dying
her dead friend
stayed with her all night.
She wore a frayed hospital gown,
and sat in a wheelchair.

She was telling her
how things are there;
how televisions don't exist;
how you can get a decent cup of tea,
and how pleased her geese were to see her.

Being there, was in fact
a lot like the old days,
except she hadn't seen
her husband,
and what a blessing that was.

By morning, Mrs Crow
had almost gone;
just a halo of silver hair remained,
and her geese were in flight
in a string of noisy beads across the sky.

The Unmade Phone Call

She hears the thin outline of her sister's voice
calling from sky above their childhood home.

She is saying how the new houses
are unbuilding themselves;
mortar divides into lime and cement
and windows turn back into sand.

And on gipsy land near the school
she can see the broken bicycles
and the unshod horses
airborn, rushing the wind.

Then she tells her
she must put down the phone.

Coming Home

(for Emma)

You disappeared slowly;
hair first, the flesh from your bones,
then you were gone
from Christmas
like a bad-taste magic trick.

When you finally died
everything electrical in your room
stopped working.
The family tried to call you up on the ouija board
but you must have been too far away.

A year later, your mother
heard you coming home
late on a Friday night;
brushing your teeth,
taking your face off, everything.

Princess of Radiation

They have decoded your blueprint,
messed up your electricity
so even your good cells
won't fit neatly inside.

At Christmas you try a small glass
of cider and a handful of sweets
but your strange new cells
rebuff these offerings.

Everyone sits round your bed
watching the ghost
of Christmas on television.
All except you wear a paper crown.

Things I Should Have Asked My Grandmother

What happened to that jar of milk teeth,
and the wine glass chockfull of feathers?

When you have two flat pieces of a doll's face,
how do you know its mouth will join up?

Where did you get that wig head
and why were its eyes always closed?

Does it mean that spring's on its way
if a bird sings from the top rung of a ladder?

And if the bunny hops free of a jelly before it's set,
what should I do with the eggs in its belly?

My Grandmother's Things

Did you see after you died
men took an inventory of your house
to find out what was valuable?

And did you notice, I wonder,
when we stripped your bed that last time,
the imprint of your body on the mattress?

I can't remember what happened
to those sheets, nor to the letters
you kept in the drawer of your dresser.

But I have your watch – a gold-plated thing
I had to stop wearing
because it stained my wrist green.

Hosanna

The pawnbroker's window
is crowded with mirrors,
with freshwater pearls
and a clock-face pushed to the glass.

My grandmother's bible
sits at the back;
pages grown together,
a palm cross locked inside.

She sings Hosanna
though she is a ghost –
a little girl in white socks –
she sings Hosanna to the Lord.

At the Bus Stop

I imagine my grandmother like me,
all dressed up with a bus to catch
locking the door behind, the scent of lavender
woken by the brush of her skirt.

I see us walking, crossing the road,
each in the others' shadow,
we take silver from our pocket
as the bus heaves into view.

Then I feel the day fall clean away
and everything is too bright to see.
My heart fights to be free of its cage,
and the bus lurches past.

We are fixed to the pavement,
our shadows circling
like carnivorous birds,
weighing up which one of us to eat first.

Dinner and Dancing with Mr Halfpenny's Cat

I see the dead walk past like a cine-projection
from the window of my childhood house:
Mr Halfpenny with his cat on a leash
taking her just as far as the corner,
old Bert with his crooked back
and the impossible weight of his shopping.

I am twelve years old and I have padded out
my bra to fit the second-hand ball-gown
bought from the hospice fête.
It is Sunday again. I watch the corner
for my grandmother – the steamed-pudding in her arms
and see the street flicker as she comes into view.

I make my entrance to suitable music
and the dead all sit on hard-back chairs,
some dolls and bears placed there, to make up the numbers.
After dinner it appears my dance-card is full –
I take to the floor with Mr Halfpenny's cat
as he shadows us slowly at the end of the leash.

The Inside-out House

The house turned inside-out,
innards tumbled onto the grass,
trees watching
with the quick eyes of birds.

One has laid eggs
in the body of her parents' bed
and is breaking them open
with a pin sharp beak.

It eats the yolk,
leaves the albumen
to dribble down
through the rusty springs.

What the House Said

When the sky feeds me birds,
I cough them up
in the middle of your parlour games.

I do not have to pretend to like you,
we have signed no contract
yet you line my insides with your lives.

When you examine them
you'll see even the most vivid
burnt crow-black.

What the Earth Said

When your feet are dirty
with ash from the hearthstones

and your rug is untidy
with the skull-bones of mice

when the snow has hidden
your path to the river

and the river's too busy
to allow you across

when the stairs have bought you
as far as the landing
lie down on me, lie down.

I am a feather in the heart of a stone
the bed you imagined
a train's distance from home.

The House of Thorns

(after Alice Maher)

It takes no more than a word
for a flame to stir in its womb
for smoke to rise and push at the walls
like a trapped and injured beast.

There is no chimney, no window,
no gasps of air, so the fire that's grown
too big for the hearth
will die before it eats up the room.

Here is a bed for the wolf,
here is a chair burst at the seams
and here's the little pot
that will cook and cook and cook.

*

It's hard to imagine a path from this house
when you can't imagine a door.
The roof is braced against all four winds,
you're swaddled inside a coat of thorns.

There are stories about spring mornings,
about dew-soaked grass,
the signature of your footsteps;
you, the only child on earth.

The house is blind to romance;
makes you pin down your tongue;
rocks you till you fall asleep
hush-a-bye, hush-a-bye, hush-a-bye.

*

When the seeds are planted
and the roses are grown
mature enough for a harvest of thorns
and all the effort of building a home
tattoos neat scratches
on your parents' hands,
now, think of a house.

Think of another house
a house of your own,
cut from the cloth of your very own skin.
The thought rises up
like a singing clock,
its bird constructed
of feathers and springs.

PART TWO

Waiting for Bluebeard

The child in the garden wears a coat
collaged from the skins of paper,
sutured with lengths of my hair.
I am inside the house
in a matching coat.

There is no one to tell us not to –
called here, as we were
by the *halloo* of peacocks
who turned tail
the day we arrived.

We are waiting for Bluebeard,
and when he happens here
in his grey-silver car,
he will unleash wolves
like rain.

The Disappearing

1

The tariff for crossing the threshold
was a single layer of skin.

She imagined a snake
unzipping itself in one deft move.

She imagined herself lithe
inside the house, her new home.

She didn't imagine the scarring
nor the painstaking care required

to leave the ghost of herself
on the doorstep like a cold-caller.

In Bluebeard's Garden

Some are only buried waist-deep
and from a distance
they are trees holding hands.

He planted them
in date order – his first love
nearest the singing grass.

He has hidden her eyes
so cannot see
himself drowned.

At the Dress Shop

At the dress shop, the assistants bustle
as Bluebeard watches from an ornate chair.

He has phoned ahead and they come at her
with his choices, all prim on wire hangers.

She parades for him and so do all the women
in the mirrors. Every one looks older than her.

She imagines being animated by Muybridge,
the drabbest dress painted onto her body;

Bluebeard at the handle of the zoetrope,
she spinning too fast for herself.

Bluebeard's Letters

The first time he left her alone
she wandered his house
in search of traces of a life before.

The stories of course, had been fixed
in her head by dress-makers' pins
since she was a girl, but this wasn't fiction.

She found nothing in his study
but the heads of his ancestors
glowering from vellum walls.

She unearthed only shadows in the library
spilled between bookcases,
soaked into the carpets like blood.

She discovered the love letters in a trunk
at the bottom of their bed
with a handful of his half-written notes.

They were pressed between skins of paper
like statice and cornflowers.
His stuttering lines were almost human.

Bluebeard's Ancestors

When she takes up his morning coffee
he isn't there for once,
just the portraits of his ancestors
who fall quiet as she taps the door.

She is familiar with the scolding
of their eyes –
they do not need to say a word
for her to burn inside her skin.

They know the coffee isn't perfect,
they've had time to refine their senses.
Maybe it's her own acrid flavour;
maybe it's the vulgar blend of beans.

The Disappearing

2

She cut her nails and filed them
so they wouldn't catch
the fine sheets of the bed.

So they wouldn't graze
exposed and tender skin.
She wasn't, after all, a beast.

And every week she'd trim them down
even though sometimes
they were not dangerous at all.

She stored clippings in a Kilner jar
and read time in them
as one might read it in a mirror.

Dog

She grew to know him by his dog;
gauged his humours
by the slant of its ears,
learnt when to keep low to the ground.

Dog preceded her by fifteen years;
every corner of the house,
every midnight walk from the pub
tattooed the map on his hide

Now, Dog was half-blind,
his teeth and claws grown dull.
She nursed him with milksop
all his last week.

When Dog died, Bluebeard sobbed,
held Dog's fading warmth to him,
murmured for hours
into Dog's empty ear.

Later she found him outside,
clay stuck to the soles of his boots
quarrying with pick and shovel,
waist deep in Dog's grave.

The Disappearing

3

One night she visited herself after death
drowned in the three-piece suit
of a very large man,
her braids held aloft by a cloud of bats.

She snipped at the lamp's fringe
with a pair of garden shears
that were too rusted
for her living hands to work.

The winter morning brought so little light
it was hard to understand
the hank of hair like a noose at rest
severed on the wooden floor.

A Week with Bluebeard

Monday – Drawing Down the Moon

He'd been calling the moon
by all of her names on his midnight walk:
Selene, Persephone, Artemis…
so she followed him home
cold light burning the back of his neck.

When the music in his head begun
he offered his arm
and they took several turns of the patio
in a stately upright manner,
till the music grew faster.

He gripped her by the waist, by the wrist,
as he spun her around.
And wolves raised their voices to the sky
and her names fell from her
and the night blurred.

Tuesday – The Brothers of the Fields

Three times he must lead the bull round the field
twice he must lead it back.
Milk and wine clink together in a bag;
honey sleeps inside the jar in his paw.

No rain in months, and the gorse is charred
by a glass-fire lit by the sun;
the ground is rent with fissures,
he sees earth right through to her burning heart.

Wednesday Is Market Day

Pigs driven inside the trailer
till it is brimful with scrubbed pink hides.
They've grown used to the singsong voice
he uses for them; are lulled
into slumber before the engine is sparked.

Each dreams its own intricate dream,
too baffling to translate into human shapes,
for pigs are wise and ancient.
And yet they feel secure in sleep
as Bluebeard steers through the darkening day.

On the other side he watches over
their sleepwalk to the slaughterhouse
like a stepfather at the school gates,
keen to vanish himself away
before one of them turns round to see.

Thursday – Thunder

She wakes early to what she thinks is thunder
but harder listening reveals Bluebeard
moving things around in the yard.

He has lit the furnace and its slit throat glows
from the corner of his workshop
where a handful of mice had nested.

The bravest sits up on its haunches,
observes Bluebeard's wide shoulders
labouring over shadows.

Only the mouse hears her come in with his tea
heaving the door just wide enough for herself,
cushioning it with her body.

Friday – The Cows.

There is something about
their breathing that pleases him.
As he presses his ear to a flank,
he hears the slow certainty
of a heartbeat, so close
it might be his own.

They are paying reverence
to the evening star;
eyes glowing like moonstones
the hay-scented clouds of their voices
sing to the glory of Venus
Oh, sister of the Earth.

He follows their slow migration
over fields all the long night,
as if wading through water
warm enough to lie down in,
to drift gently to sleep in,
to be free of his name.

Saturday – Harvest Day

Then one Saturday, when he was at harvest
there came a knock at the door *rat-a-tat-tat*
and a stranger stood on the path.

She spied him from the window, a young man
tall as Bluebeard, nearly as broad,
a deep scar cleaved from his ear to his throat.

His eyes skimmed the windows,
did he notice the twitch of a curtain;
did he sense a stifled heartbeat in the house?

Bluebeard had told her his children were dead,
yet this stranger was not all that strange;
the blood-copper hair, the ice-grey eyes.

She thought of their baby-pictures in the hallway
all seven, fat as calves, in seven silver-cross prams,
then she thought of the sickle in Bluebeard's hand.

Sunday – Postprandial Music

After lunch, Bluebeard retires to his study
and she is alone with the dishes.
She fills up the sink with too hot water,
till her hands burn scarlet.

The grease melts easily
and soon the crockery squeaks white again;
drying on the rack, china plates are moons
awakened by the noonday sun.

Sunday is music day, and by and by
a soprano will bleed through the walls
and Bluebeard will wail and sob
like a wolf in the jaws of a trap.

Child

She must have been somewhere else
when they cut her open, hauled the baby out
and tried to zip her up like an empty bag.

She must have been waiting for a bus,
or playing lawn tennis, she must have been
Atargis the mermaid goddess at the boating lake.

That night, cries rose from her half-closed wound
and they watched her temperature soar –
mapping it on a chart like the lunatic flight of a moth.

She awoke as a rock in a fast-moving river.
There was no child, no tiny warmth.
There were voices and hands, all of them hollow.

The Disappearing

4

She stepped out of herself
like a matryoshka, one full moon,
looked along the row of herself,
at the hand-painted colours,
checked each pair of eyes
for what lived there.

A scarf hung about each pelvic girdle
to conceal the scar of each birth.
Hearts were black hens
held in each pair of arms
and cabbages grew
from fallen seeds at their feet.

When earth spun away from the moon
she attempted to gather herself back in,
and when she could not
she drowned the sun like a sack of kittens
and threaded the rooster's song
back into his throat.

Rabbit Season

Woken by the sharp burn
of moonlight on her face
she moves to the window,
sees searchlights unearthing
the season's rabbits,
then remembers the child.

The last time she'd gone out
she lost her slippers in the river
so now her bare feet carry her
down the stairs, along the hallway
over the patio and into a night
cut with gunshot.

She digs at the edge of the lawn
with a spade first,
then with her hands
to be closer to her work.
By dawn, there are little mounds of earth,
but still no child.

She tidies herself up in time
to make Bluebeard's porridge.
She watches him emerge from the fields
his mossy boots soaked with dew,
a string of rabbit pelts at his waist;
all their open eyes.

Bluebeard's Music

When Bluebeard played the piano
moonlight leached through the curtains
and stained his hands
with its haunted blood.

All of the notes were stillborn;
scraps of birds
that fell into the air
all feather, no heartbeat.

On those nights, the sky was vast
and she pretended to sleep,
the empty cave of her body
shored against its own breathing.

Bluebeard at Night

When she's gone to bed
Bluebeard sobs like a wolf
from his leather armchair.

Only the television responds,
slips the leash of its power cable,
dragging itself to its master's heel.

She hears them leave the house
like solemn drinking partners
emptied into the night at closing time.

Then she imagines the nocturnal insects
entering the house by the grace
of the left-open door

and their frantic gathering
round the hallway's
false moon.

The Disappearing

5

Each day a new birdskin appeared on the patio
emptied of its heart and bones and singing.
Perhaps it was the owl's meticulous work.

When she'd harvested enough skins,
she sat at her table one morning
and fashioned herself a birdskin coat.

And when she put it on, the uncured hide
grafted easily to her own skin.
And when she tried to sing, she could not.

Bluebeard at Work

She has grown into her own company;
no longer looks in cupboards for the child,
moves through rooms so silently,
she could be a ghost.

Bluebeard is at his leather desk
engaged in the routine of – what exactly?
She doesn't know what keeps him
occupied and furious.

She has learnt to keep herself so neat and tidy
she corresponds exactly to her shadow;
no untidy edges,
no hanging threads, no singing.

Bluebeard at the Bookshop

He moves through the shelves
like night through water,
eyes cast over broken spines.

He full-stops at 'O',
draws out a skin-bound volume
with red arabesques.

There are no fellow browsers
to hear the half-human cries
as he lets it fall open.

Mermaids, dog-headed men
and unblinking serpents
meet his gaze from the pages.

He closes it quickly, removes to the counter,
carries out the transaction
with a handful of silver.

The Disappearing

6

She presses missed heartbeats
into a wet plaster wall
with her wedding-ring finger
measuring out silences
wide enough to fall into.

Plaster loses its flesh-tone
when it dries,
leeches moisture from skin.
The heart dives
into a well of forgetting.

In Bluebeard's Kitchen

Ten years of bones from his table
worried of flesh; each one stored in the pantry
once she'd scoured them deliciously white.

Skin beetles are efficient housewives,
she indulged them with handfuls of moths
and feathers to pepper their diet.

Skulls are awkward; brain-matter
whipped like eggs then flushed down the sink
till the water runs clear.

But she cannot remove
his marrow-deep tooth-marks
scored like a tally down the longest bones.

The Disappearing

7

She already knew her bones
were there for all the world to see,
so she unpeeled her hide
in the changing rooms.

Bluebeard barely recognised
the small neat form
slicing through the footbath
like a fox through night.

In the pool, she was an electric storm
and the water shrunk away.
She marvelled, *oh the joy!*
she could not feel a thing.

Bluebeard the Chef

You coax the rabbit from its skin,
cradle the bruised flesh ripped with shot.
A deft incision and soon the tiny heart
is in your hand, its stillness
opens up a dark hole in the sky for you.

You climb inside
and all the stars are dying eyes
fixed into you like pins.
So you slice each optic nerve
and disappear.

The knife completes your hand
with such sweet eloquence
you part recall its amputation
when you were wordless
in your father's house.

The Disappearing

8

And by teatime she couldn't recognise
a single hair on her head.
Her heart was a metal bucket
and her eyes were the spaces
where fish bowls had sat.

She talked to the chickens
and the guinea fowl and the pheasants
in the fields as she fed them.
She had inherited their scratchy voices;
the urge to look over their shoulders.

Nothing they could say
would set her mind at rest.
None of them knew of a road outside,
they all said they were born here;
perhaps she was too.

Liminal

She has forgotten how to sleep;
covets the house's slowed breathing
its routine loosening of joints.

Cats are singing
in their extraordinary voices
to the moon or whoever will listen.

Angels are unzipping the sky
and she pictures herself
black-feathered, hollow-boned.

There is a fire on the other side
of the city, there is a taxi waiting
at the end of the drive.

Grass

All summer grass had grown
around them like a lake:
crickets harangued from the windowsills,
field mice drew closer to the walls
and a mute swan clung to the roof.

And through all the long days
Bluebeard held to his desk
like a drowning man,
with the green-grass light
stopped fast by the curtains.

The mower was broken,
the scythe was unwieldy
so it was just easier this way;
to let grass take the house
to sail it away, she'd decided.

Bluebeard and the Wolves

The sun grown too heavy
came to rest at the edge of your land,
so you went out to meet it
with a bottle of wine.

Then poured out two mugs
drank them both down,
and cast the empty bottle into the river
like a hollowed-out fish.

You dropped to all fours,
dug at the earth with your paws
as a circle of wolves grew around
with night at their backs.

You held a swaddled form aloft
in your jaws, then took off
with your howling entourage
into the oil-dark plain of the sky.

The Disappearing

9

This time the door wasn't locked
so she saw the room's plunder
floating in the dark liquid
of neatly labelled jars –
fingernails, tangles of hair,
an unborn child.

My skin hung from a wire hanger
on the back of the door
like a wedding dress
emptied of its bride.
It was too tight to climb into,
so she left the house naked.

Hide

My father made me a dress
from patches of sky
on my mother's old sewing machine.
He stitched them together
with lengths of her hair
and carved all the buttons
from her neat white teeth
but I would not give him my heart.

My father made me a dress
from the light of the moon
pinned into place
with her fine finger bones.
He made me a dress as bright as the sun
and sewed her gold wedding ring
into the hem
but I would not give him my hand.

My father offered me
the pelt of his dog —
how quickly his knife
freed that beast from its skin.
I climbed inside while it was still warm,
zipped it up tight
then walked into the fire
so he could not give me his love.

ACKNOWLEDGEMENTS

Acknowledgements are due to the editors of the following publications in which some of these poems first appeared: *Ambit*, BigCityLit.com, *The Bow Wow Shop*, *Epicentre Magazine*, *Horizon Review*, *Interlitq*, *London Grip*, *Magma*, *Mslexia*, *nthposition*, *Peony Moon*, *Poetry International*, *Poetry Review*, *Poetry Salzburg Review*, *Peony Moon*, *Seam*, *Silk Road Review* and *Smith's Knoll*, 'The Disappearing' was performed at Wymondham Words in September 2012.

I would also like to thank George Szirtes and Neil Astley for their continuing support of my work and to thank my workshop group, who saw earlier drafts of some of these poems: Jo Guthrie, Andrea Holland, Matthew Howard, Andrew McDonnell and Esther Morgan. I would like to thank Penelope Shuttle, William Bedford and Padrika Tarrant for their encouragement and support. Thanks are due also to Chris Gribble at Writers Centre Norwich for sage advice, and to Arts Council England for financial support. I would like to extend my thanks to everybody who has ever liked my poems. And finally I would like to thank my husband, the poet Martin Figura for everything and everything else.